Arise
AND
GO BACK

A Journey Through Grief, Grace and Restoration

Adiese Jonas-Murphy

ARISE AND GO BACK. Copyright © 2025. Adiese Jonas-Murphy. All Rights Reserved.

Printed in the United States of America.

No portion of this book may be reproduced, stored in a retrieval system, or transmitted in any form or by any means, except for brief quotations in printed reviews, without the prior written permission of DayeLight Publishers or Adiese Jonas-Murphy.

ISBN: 978-1-966723-40-0 (paperback)

Scripture quotations marked "KJV" are taken from the Holy Bible, King James Version (Public Domain).

Scripture quotations marked (NIV) are taken from the Holy Bible, New International Version®, NIV®. Copyright © 1973, 1978, 1984 by Biblica, Inc." Used by permission of Zondervan. All rights reserved worldwide.

Scripture quotations marked (NLT) are taken from the Holy Bible, New Living Translation, copyright © 1996, 2004, 2007 by Tyndale House Foundation. Used by permission of Tyndale House Publishers, Inc., Carol Stream, Illinois 60188. All rights reserved.

Scripture quotations marked "NKJV" are taken from the New King James Version. Copyright © 1982 by Thomas Nelson, Inc. Used by permission. All rights reserved. Bible text from the New King James Version® is not to be reproduced in copies or otherwise by any means except as permitted in writing by Thomas Nelson, Inc., Attn: Bible Rights and Permissions, P.O. Box 141000, Nashville, TN 37214-1000.

Scripture quotations marked "ESV" are from the ESV Bible® (The Holy Bible, English Standard Version®), copyright © 2001 by Crossway Bibles, a publishing ministry of Good News Publishers. Used by permission. All rights reserved.

DEDICATION

I dedicate this book to the hearts of women who feel forgotten, bitter, or broken.

Arise and Go Back: A Journey Through Grief, Grace and Restoration is designed to help you rediscover the God who still writes beautiful endings, even after the worst beginnings.

As women, we are symbols of stability and inner strength. We are expected to hold families, ministries, and communities together, even while carrying unimaginable personal loss. I am giving you permission to feel by offering you a sacred space to grieve with honesty and hope. Naomi's journey speaks directly to the emotional, spiritual, and social grief that we women face:

- The loss of a spouse.
- The loss of a child/children.
- The loss of our own bodies.

- The identity crisis that follows from new and emerging seasons of our lives.
- The tension between bitterness and belief.

Her story mirrors what many modern women carry silently.

Alongside Naomi's story, I present to you my experiences made public for the first time: real, raw, and redeemed. I've started this path, and God met me in it. The world says, "get over it," but scripture shows us how to go through it. You can live more than a half-life. There's no need to get stuck in the pause between pain and purpose. Welcome to an altar where you can meet God again in the ashes of what you've lost.

ACKNOWLEDGEMENTS

This book was written in the shadows of grief, but also in the light of God's grace.

To my heavenly Father God, who never left me without His presence, thank You. You sat with me in my periods of silence and waiting, and whispered, "Arise" when all I wanted to do was hide. These pages belong to You.

To my husband, Darren; we've faced our fair share of uninvited grief, yet through it all, God has not let us go. I'm thankful for His redemption and favor that rests upon us. The testimonies entrusted to us will be a legacy of how our union stood up to some of the difficult tests of time. Thank you for your 'Ruth-like' commitment through the wreckage, without asking me to rush through it.

To my beautiful children, Zachary and Dominique, your laughter, innocence, and joy gave me life on days I felt lost. Thank you for reminding me that even in sorrow, purpose still lives, moves, and breathes. You are symbols of God's love, grace, and favor in my life.

To my mother, Janett, whose strength is a force to be reckoned with; thank you for teaching me how to be fragile and fierce. I am so grateful for the life lessons you have taught me.

To my father (deceased), your absence left an unimaginable void in my life, but your love planted roots in me that have kept me grounded to this day. I carry your blood and strength with every word I write.

To my incredible sister, Shermaine, whose recent fight for life inspired mine; you are living proof that God still performs miracles. Your strength reminds me that hope lives, even in the midst of chaos, pain, and death.

To my brother-in-law, Orlando, you stood by like an unwavering pillar beside my sister during a time when chaos threatened to unravel everything. Your loyalty and compassion are etched into the fabric of this journey.

To my mother-in-law, Sydna, who faced stage four cancer with courage and grace, and to my father-in-law,

Dorrell, whose own diagnosis rocked our family; thank you for teaching me what faith looks like in the fire.

To my cousin, Amadi, extended family, close friends, and intercessors, you saw me when I couldn't see myself. Thank you for covering me in prayer, letting me grieve without judgment, and speaking life over me when I was too tired to hope.

To my church family, many of you are just now learning about my story. This is your shepherdess being open and honest with her emotions. Thank you for allowing me space to serve you while still healing. You made room for both the minister and the grieving woman.

And to you, dear reader, if you've picked up this book while walking through your own grief, please know this: your pain is seen. This book is not just mine. It belongs to every woman who has smiled through sorrow, stayed silent in suffering, and dared to hope again.

Thank you for letting me rise with you.

Arising is not forgetting.
It is remembering with hope!

Going back is not retreating,
It is rediscovering the past
and returning to the God
who still writes beauty from ashes.

TABLE OF CONTENTS

Dedication iii

Acknowledgements v

Preface 13

Introduction 17

Chapter One: Delayed Grief 21

Chapter Two: The Unsettling Providence of God (Part 1) 25

Chapter Three: The Unsettling Providence of God (Part 2) 29

Chapter Four: Grief: A Prophetic Pivot 33

Chapter Five: Whispered Words: 'Arise & Go Back' 39

Chapter Six: Bitter, Not Broken 45

Chapter Seven: God's Pattern of Provision 49

Chapter Eight: God in the Gleaning 55

Chapter Nine: Finding Love Again 59

Chapter Ten: God's Favor and Deliverance 65

Chapter Eleven: A Grieving Mother's Legacy 69

Chapter Twelve: The Witness of Sacred Scars 73

Chapter Thirteen: Beauty After 'Mara' 77

About the Author 81

PREFACE

Grief has a way of unmaking us. Yes, I did say unmaking. It strips us of what we held dear, rewrites our stories without our permission, and leaves us holding the pieces of a life we no longer recognize.

When I revisited Naomi's story in the Book of Ruth some time ago, I didn't just read about a woman in mourning. I saw myself through this widow who endured significant loss and hardships in quick succession. I further saw myself in this same woman who renamed herself "Mara" (meaning bitter) because she could not reconcile her faith with her pain.

Naomi's story is far from a fairytale. I like that. It is raw, human, and holy. It is the story of a woman who lost nearly everything: her home, her husband, her sons, her hope, and still found her way back, not to what was, but to the God who never left her.

This book is in no way a theological exposition. It is a heart-to-heart reflection of Naomi's pain and mine; an acknowledgement of the grief I delayed for years, a companion guide, especially for women finding themselves suddenly thrust into grief's arms. Many people who have faced grief deeply have also doubted God's goodness in the dark. They wonder if healing is still possible after loss.

Arise and Go Back is a call, a recall, and comfort. It is the invitation that God gave to Naomi when the famine ended in the 'House of Bread.' It is the same invitation that He gives to us today; not to erase our grief, but to rise in it. Our return, then, is not just geographical but spiritual; to the presence of a God who restores and redeems us.

Each chapter is laced with my reflections, biblical insights, and guidance for those who are navigating the valley of loss. My prayer is that as you journey through these pages, you'll not only see Naomi, you will see yourself. And more than that, you'll see God, the One who redeems bitter seasons and writes a legacy through loss.

If you're holding this book with a heavy heart, may I encourage you? You don't have to have it all together.

Arise and Go Back

You don't even need to feel strong. All you need to do is arise and go back to God.

INTRODUCTION

Grief is no respecter of timing, titles, or temperament. It doesn't pause for ministry schedules, work calendars, family responsibilities, or any other perfectly laid-out plans. It simply does not wait for you to be ready. It just comes… unannounced, uninvited, and in waves you never expected to survive.

I didn't set out to write a book on my own silent journey with grief. Why would I want to make this struggle public? It really doesn't make sense! I simply wrote because I needed to survive it.

When I lost my father, something massive shifted inside of me. A silence I had never known settled over my soul, and I didn't know how to process it. After all, Dad died exactly one week after I gave birth to Zachary, my first child. I was caught standing between life and death. On one hand, I embraced joyful expressions of congratulatory messages welcoming Zachary into the world, **but** on the other hand, I struggled to accept the sorrowful tones of condolences that issued the separation that death brings to its loved ones. It was an awful place to be.

I made it through the funeral. Then, it was time for motherhood. The only way I knew how to survive was to suppress my grief.

Life happened in full force. The demands of work, church, and other duties poured in.

Then came my mother's stroke, and watching her fight to live as she once had. This was another kind of loss I was unprepared to confront.

While grappling with the now-mounting layers of loss, my sister's near-death experience shook the ground beneath my feet. It created an avalanche filled with fear and anxiety that I was facing for the very first time.

My story is not quite done! In the middle of facing my sister's trying test, came the words "stage four cancer" for my mother-in-law; this added another layer of ache that still lingers to this day. Then, as if my heart wasn't already full of fear, we learned a couple of weeks later that my father-in-law also faced a stage four cancer diagnosis.

Talk about crashing waves of grief showing up at my door! Never mind the door, it blew my entire house down!

In all of this, life kept moving. I had to keep going.

As a product of Caribbean descent, a pastor's wife, a mother, minister, and media practitioner, I felt I needed to stay strong, keep smiling, and show up. But inside? Man, oh man, I was unraveling.

This book is the story of that 'unraveling' and the rising that came after. It is a journey through Naomi's story in the Book of Ruth and how her grief became my mirror. Naomi didn't just suffer loss; she was a woman who gave language to bitterness, who knew what it meant to return empty, and who eventually discovered that God writes redemption into even the most broken chapters.

Arise and Go Back: A Journey Through Grief, Grace and Restoration is an invitation to be honest about your pain, and wrestle with questions that hold grief and faith in the same trembling hands. Together we will walk with

Naomi, not just through her pain, but toward the promise.

Ready to journey with me? Let's turn to the next page.

CHAPTER ONE

DELAYED GRIEF

"The Long Silence Before the Storm"

"Why my soul, are you downcast? Why so disturbed within me? Put your hope in God, for I will yet praise Him my Savior and my God."
Psalm 42:5 (NIV)

As I watched his coffin being lowered into the earth, I suddenly confronted the reality that death had caused a painful separation that I still haven't fully processed. I walked away from the graveside and headed back to my vehicle. My son and husband patiently awaited my return. As I entered the car and held my 4-week-old baby boy, there was no room for grief. I was now a new mom with blinkers on and whose singular focus was to provide support for this little life that depended on me. We slowly drove out of the cemetery, and the words I told myself then linger to this day: *"All is well. We got through the funeral. We buried him."*

But the truth is, I buried him deeply.

Years had passed, and I convinced myself that time had healed all my wounds, even without personally trying to be healed. I convinced myself that I had somehow dealt with the emotions that floated to the surface each time the subject of his death came up. I further thought that if I could muster up enough courage to have conversations about dad without crying, it meant that I had grieved.

I was wrong.

I pushed my grief aside to survive. It worked for a while... years to be exact. Grief sat in the background, like a heavy stone at the bottom of my soul, untouched and undisturbed, until one day, it began to rise. It wasn't that single event that broke the dam. It was a series of them experienced in quick succession:

- My mother's stroke.
- My sister's medical tragedy.
- My mother-in-law's cancer diagnosis.
- My father-in-law's cancer diagnosis.
- The sudden death of a beloved colleague.

One diagnosis after another among my network of close family and friends: cancer, heart issues, health scares. These unrelenting waves of loss all brought me back to that first wound that was never resolved. It had been seven years since I lost my father—seven years since I gave birth to my son in the middle of death's shadow. Seven years since I swallowed the weight of it all just to keep going. Now, the grief I had delayed came crashing through.

I couldn't pray it away. I couldn't organize it away. I couldn't lead others while leaking silently on the inside.

This was my 'Mara' moment. Bitterness didn't announce itself with rage. It crept in through my body, through unannounced and frequent anxiety stomach aches, heaviness in my chest, sleepless nights, emotional numbness, and a crushing sense of unprocessed sorrow. In all of this, I realized that I had never truly returned from Moab. Like Naomi, I moved there to survive. But now, I had to go back to where God's provision was. I had to go back to the places I buried the pain; not to stay there, but to finally grieve.

CHAPTER TWO

THE UNSETTLING PROVIDENCE OF GOD (PART 1)

"When the Bottom Falls Out"

"And Mahlon and Chilion died also both of them; and the woman was left of her two sons and her husband."
Ruth 1:5 (KJV)

There are moments when life stops making sense, and God's silence feels louder than any storm. Life unravels when you least expect it, and sometimes the God you trust, the One you serve, love, and lean on, feels like the same one allowing it all to happen.

That's uncomfortable.

Grief didn't knock politely on Naomi's door. It barged in, uninvited and unrelenting! Naomi, whose name meant "pleasant," returned to Bethlehem shattered and broken. Her husband and both sons were buried in Moab. Her arms hung empty. Her identity had changed. She looked at her life and said, *"Don't call me Naomi, call me Mara, because the Almighty has dealt very bitterly with me" (Ruth 1:20 – NKJV)*. How easy it is for us in our grief to blame God when things go wrong? The very things that are sometimes because of our own decisions.

As I read her story while facing my own losses, I began to understand her in a way I never had before. I too was unsettled by God's providence.

- Why would a loving, powerful God allow so many heavy blows sequentially?
- Why would He stay silent when Naomi obviously needed Him loud?
- Why does He stay silent when we at times need Him to be loud?

My unsettling grew. But in the midst of it, something holy was beginning to stir inside of me.

Prayer For When the Bottom Falls Out in Our Lives

Dear God,

I didn't see this coming. The ground beneath me has given way, and I'm free-falling through the pieces of a life I once recognized. Hold me, Lord, when everything else lets go. In Jesus' name. Amen.

Reflection Question

When everything around you feels like it's collapsing, what truth about God do you still choose to hold on to and why?

Journal Your Thoughts

_____

_____

_____

_____

_____

Adiese Jonas-Murphy

CHAPTER THREE

THE UNSETTLING PROVIDENCE OF GOD (PART 2)

"Trusting the God Who Allows"

"Then she arose with her daughters-in-law that she might return from the country of Moab…"
Ruth 1:6 (NKJV)

What do you do when the God you love allows the very things you begged Him to prevent? That's the question Naomi's life began to answer, and the one I found myself asking in my quiet moments.

Naomi's story does not begin with peace and plenty. It opens with famine, displacement, and loss. She leaves home with a husband and two sons, and over the course of a decade, returns with none. She returns to Bethlehem, worn, weathered, and renamed. Her grief was so consuming that it changed how she identified herself; not as Naomi, but 'Mara.' Not pleasant, but bitter. It wasn't that she stopped believing in God. She simply no longer recognized His goodness in her story. And I fully understand that, too.

Grief didn't just touch my life, it tore through it. And as each wave came, I wondered if the same God who had once comforted me was now the one allowing me to be undone. That is the unsettling part of providence.
We talk about God's sovereignty with reverence when things are going well. But what about when His sovereign will includes heartbreak? What about when His plan allows for the very thing that you prayed against?

Naomi had no idea that Ruth would cling to her. She had no vision of Boaz, no understanding that redemption was quietly walking toward her, even as she limped toward home. All she had was a whisper, *"Bethlehem had bread again,"* and a choice to stay in Moab or to go back home.

She chose to arise.

She got up with bitter tears, broken faith, and returned to the place she once knew; to the One she once knew, even though it didn't promise answers. Her only hope was that of survival. Her one act of obedience, however small, opened the door for restoration, legacy, redemption, and divine fulfillment.

Naomi's experiences are not about perfectly wrapped healing or spiritual clichés. It is about raw faith; the kind that keeps breathing when all feels lost. It's about the quiet courage it takes to keep walking with God, even when He feels distant. It's about the tender mercy that meets us after we've given up on understanding Him.

I am walking this journey with you, not as someone who has figured it all out, but as a woman who knows what it means to be stripped down by sorrow and simultaneously held up by grace. Trust that even in the most unsettling seasons, God is not absent; He is simply working in ways we don't yet understand.

Prayer For Trusting God in His Unsettling Providence

Dear Lord,

There are times when Your ways confuse me, when Your silence is louder than my prayers, and when Your providence feels more like punishment than protection. Give me the strength to walk the road of return. May Your providence, though unsettling, lead me into Your perfect plan. In Jesus' name. Amen.

Reflection Question

Can you recall a time when God's plan felt confusing, even painful, yet, looking back, you now see His hand? How did that season shape you?

Journal Your Thoughts

___

___

___

___

___

___

___

CHAPTER FOUR

GRIEF: A PROPHETIC PIVOT

"Call me Mara, for the Almighty has dealt very bitterly with me."
Ruth 1:20 (NKJV)

I used to think grief was only about loss; a finality that carves itself into your soul. But somewhere along my journey, I began to see another side to it: a side more glorious and meaningful. Grief acts as a prophetic pivot. What do I mean by that? Sometimes, it does not simply point backward to what has been lost, but forward to what is coming.

Grief has a way of whispering things unseen, preparing your spirit before your mind can catch up.

In my case, Dad's death was quick. His cancer diagnosis came just three weeks before his death. At thirty-six weeks pregnant and looking forward to my baby's entrance into this world, there was hardly enough time to process my new reality. My heart broke, and for me, that was the end of that chapter. Little did I know that it was also the beginning of something else.

I didn't know it at the time, but God was planting seeds through my pain; seeds I would only recognize years later when my life began to shift in ways I couldn't explain. Perhaps He is doing the same in your painful situation. Perhaps He is, right now, nurturing seeds and tilling the soil comprised of your most painful experiences.

Naomi's story in the book of Ruth is a perfect example. She lost her husband and two sons, a devastation that stripped her of security, identity, and future. Yet, that very loss drove her back to Bethlehem, where God was already orchestrating redemption through Ruth and Boaz. Her grief wasn't just a tragedy; in this case, it was a prophetic pivot, pushing her into position for the blessing she could not yet see.

I've learned that grief can act as a prophetic pivot in three ways:

1. Grief as a Forerunner

There are times when grief comes before the full storm breaks. It feels heavy, but you can't quite name why. For me, it was the season before my mother's stroke. I didn't know the details, but I felt a deep, unsettling sorrow that made me pray more earnestly. It was as though the Spirit was preparing my heart, not to remove the pain, but to anchor me before the waves hit.

Sometimes, what we call "premature" grief is God giving us an advance warning so we can fortify our faith before the test.

2. Grief as a Teacher

Grief can also show us where our foundations are weak. It strips away the comfortable illusions we hold about ourselves, others, or even God. When my colleague, Andre Wallace, passed days after his birthday, it wasn't just sorrow that I felt. It was the reopening of wounds I had never let God fully heal. My grief wasn't just about his death; it was about my own unresolved losses.

The prophetic part of that moment was this: God was showing me that unhealed grief will rise again until it is faced. He was inviting me to stop patching my soul with busyness and finally let Him touch the deep places.

3. Grief as a Midwife

I've come to see that some grief gives birth to a calling. How ironic it was that I faced grief just after giving birth!

Grief does not give birth to a calling that you celebrate with balloons and flowers. It gives birth to a calling you receive with trembling hands because it feels too heavy to carry. My own ministry to the brokenhearted was not born in the joy of answered prayers, but in the ashes of unanswered ones.

Naomi's journey back to Bethlehem was not only about survival, but it was also about being in the right place for Ruth to meet Boaz. Naomi's presence served as a midwife, connecting these two precious lives for a lifetime. Naomi's grief carried a prophetic assignment: *she was to help usher in a future she would never fully see.*

In my own life, I now realize that my grief positioned me to speak into the lives of others walking through shadows. It gives me credibility I never wanted, but God knew I would need.

Reflection Questions

If you find yourself in a season where grief feels heavier than the moment seems to justify, pause and ask:

- Is God preparing me for something ahead?
- Is He revealing something I've ignored?
- Is He birthing something through this pain?

Grief does not always tell you what's next, but it will often shape you for it. If Naomi had stayed in Moab, she would have missed the harvest. If I had stayed in my own self-protective denial, I would have missed the deeper healing and the ministry that God was calling me to.

Prayer For Grief: The Prophetic Pivot

Lord, when grief comes, help me to see beyond the loss into Your greater purpose. Teach me to discern when sorrow is not just about the past, but about the future You are shaping. May I not waste my prophetic grief, but let it position me for Your perfect will.

Journal Your Thoughts

_____

_____

Adiese Jonas-Murphy

CHAPTER FIVE

WHISPERED WORDS: 'ARISE & GO BACK'

"...The Lord had visited His people by giving them bread...."
Ruth 1:6 (NKJV)

There comes a moment after loss when everything falls silent. The funeral ends. The phone calls come to a slow halt. The frequent prayers once poured over you for strength fade gently into the background. You're left alone with the stillness of what's no longer there, and the silence feels louder than grief itself. But it is often in that silence that a whisper rises.

For Naomi, that whisper came in a simple report: *"The Lord had visited His people by giving them bread." (Ruth 1:6 - NKJV)*. No booming voice from heaven. No burning bush. Just a word passed along that something had shifted back in Bethlehem.

Bread. Life. Movement.

Having buried her husband and both sons in Moab, Naomi had every reason to settle there in sorrow and to plant her tent in the land of loss. But something in her stirred. Perhaps it was desperation. Maybe a flicker of hope. It was the still, small whisper of God saying, *"You don't have to stay here."*

That whisper was familiar to me, too. It was years later, after the dust had settled, that I felt the ache deep in my bones. So, I sought help. I signed up for Christian therapy.

Each experience of loss carved a hollow space in me. Grief, now complicated, had layered itself over my soul like heavy blankets, and I couldn't seem to throw them off. But in the stillness, when no one was watching, God began to whisper: *"Get up, Adiese. Not to forget, but to continue."*

The whisper didn't erase the pain. It didn't undo my losses. But it gently invited me out of the place of paralysis. Like Naomi, I was being called to arise and go back; not just geographically, but spiritually and emotionally.

Grief has a way of making us want to retreat. To go silent. To stay in Moab, where it's familiar, even if painful. But there is always a "Bethlehem" in the distance; a place of true provision, though it may not appear to be so. Bethlehem reminds us that God is still at work, even when our lives feel empty.

Let's shine the spotlight on Naomi's journey back. It wasn't triumphant. It was quite weary. She had no guarantees, no sons, no money, and no clear plan. Just Ruth beside her and a distant hope that Bethlehem might offer something; anything better than Moab.

Your journey may feel like that too. You may not feel strong. You may not know what tomorrow holds. But sometimes, all God requires is a "yes" to His whisper, and a willingness to get up, even if your steps are slow, even if your heart is still broken.

What Naomi didn't know was that her return would unlock redemption. The same town where she once felt empty would become the backdrop for Ruth's love story and the birthplace of a lineage that would lead to King David and ultimately to Jesus. The whisper to arise and go back wasn't about reclaiming the past; it was about participating in the future; a future unknown to Naomi and a future unknown to you.

Sometimes grief convinces us that our best days are behind us, that we're too wounded to hope again. But God's whisper tells a different story. It says: *"There is still life. There is still bread. There is still purpose."*

Prayer For The Whisper "Arise and Go Back"

Merciful Savior,

In the stillness of my sorrow, help me to hear You. When the noise of grief drowns out Your voice, when loss feels louder than love, and when the ache of what I have buried keeps me bound, whisper again. In Jesus' Name. Amen.

Reflection Question

What quiet whisper or gentle nudge from God have you been ignoring?

Journal Your Thoughts

CHAPTER SIX

BITTER, NOT BROKEN

"...Do not call me Naomi; call me Mara..."
Ruth 1:20 (NKJV)

As Naomi walked into Bethlehem, the town stirred because of her. Grief had aged her, and pain had reshaped her countenance. The woman who once walked away full had come back empty, and she didn't try to hide it. *But she said to them, "Do not call me Naomi; call me Mara, for the Almighty has dealt very bitterly with me. (Ruth 1:20 – NKJV).*

Naomi wasn't being dramatic. She was being honest...bitterly honest! And sometimes honesty in grief sounds like bitterness. There is a weight to loss that doesn't sit quietly. It groans. It aches. It changes how you speak and how you see the world. When you've buried dreams and unmet expectations, stood at gravesides, or watched someone you love suffer in ways you couldn't fix, bitterness can seep in; not necessarily as hatred toward God, but as a sign of deep, unresolved pain.

In moments of deep solitude and sorrow, I have felt 'Mara' rise in my chest. It's easy to assume that our feelings of bitterness mean that we've failed in faith, trust, and surrender to God. But Naomi's story shows us otherwise. Naomi was bitter, yes, but she *still* walked back to Bethlehem. She *still* brought Ruth with her. She *still* moved.

Naomi's transparency about her bitterness ultimately led her to a place of healing; a place you can arrive at too. Bitterness didn't break her faith; it simply revealed the depth of her sorrow. It showed that she had lost something so precious that it shook her to the core. That kind of bitterness doesn't always mean a heart turned from God; sometimes it can mean a heart wrestling with God.

And God can handle that.

He didn't rebuke Naomi for her honesty. He didn't silence her lament. He simply met her in her pain, and quietly, redemptively, began to weave beauty back into her broken story. Isn't that just like God?

You may be carrying bitterness right now over the partner you lost, the child you buried, the divorce that shook your core, the diagnosis that came too soon, the betrayal that you never saw coming, or the friend you couldn't save. Maybe you feel guilty for the way it still hurts. But hear this, friend, bitter doesn't always mean broken. It means you've been through something real. It means your love ran deep, and your soul remembers what it lost.

And that is okay.

The enemy would have you believe that grief makes you useless and that God can't work with your sorrow, but Naomi's life proves otherwise. Her bitterness didn't disqualify her. It was the soil where God's mercy bloomed. Why not bring your *'Mara'* to God? You can be honest about how much it hurts.

And you can still rise.

Prayer: Bitter, Not Broken

Gracious Father,

I come to You carrying what's too heavy to hold. Bitterness has crept into places joy once lived. I place my weary heart into Your hands and say even now: *"Do with me what only You can."* In Jesus' Name. Amen.

Reflection Question

In what ways has bitterness tried to define your story?

Journal Your Thoughts

_____

_____

_____

_____

_____

_____

_____

_____

_____

CHAPTER SEVEN

GOD'S PATTERN OF PROVISION

"But Ruth replied, 'Don't urge me to leave you or to turn back from you. Where you go I will go, and where you stay I will stay. Your people will be my people and your God my God.'"
Ruth 1:16 (NIV)

Naomi was grieving a husband. Ruth was also grieving a husband. Two women, two losses, but one thread of providence held them together as they grieved. Have you ever found yourself connected to someone by the thread of grief? Grief has a way of isolating us, yet in Naomi and Ruth's case, it became the soil in which faith, loyalty, and redemption would take root.

Their pain was raw and real, and their return to Bethlehem was met with hopelessness. Ruth and Naomi are symbols of you, me, and all of humanity: a hopeless case journeying, had it not been for our Savior, Jesus Christ, who entered the picture. But even before either woman knew the depths of sorrow that they would walk through, God had already planted provision in their path.

When Ruth said, *"Where you go, I will go... your people will be my people and your God my God" (see Ruth 1:16)*, she wasn't only being loyal to Naomi. She took on a divine assignment, and her presence in Naomi's life would become the conduit through which hope, legacy, and deliverance for the human race would come. She renounced the polytheistic practices of her culture and identity and embraced Naomi's God as her God. Ruth took on Naomi's hopelessness and became the answer to a prayer that Naomi had not yet prayed.

Notice, it was not Naomi who asked Ruth to stay. In fact, she tried to send her away. Her heart was too broken to see the blessing standing beside her. But God's favor doesn't require our awareness to operate. It simply moves, silently, sovereignly, ahead of us.

God gave Naomi Ruth (loyal, brave, and obedient) not when she realized she needed her, but before the famine, the funerals, and the fallen tears. God quite often sends people into our lives who will one day carry us when we can't walk. He allows us to build relationships that will later become our bridges over 'bitter' waters. It's amazing how He prepares for our rescue, while we're still dancing and unaware.

Throughout scripture, we see this pattern of God's provision ahead of pain. Here are a few examples to strengthen this point:

- God created Eve before Adam knew loneliness.

- God placed a ram in the thicket before Abraham raised the knife to kill Isaac.

- God called Joseph to Egypt ahead of his brothers to preserve them in famine.

- God sent Jesus before we even knew we needed saving.

It is God's character to go before us. He is not reactive, but proactive. He doesn't wait for us to break before He begins to build.

As you read this book, I want you to know that your provision is already in motion, while your pain may be on the horizon. This is not always visible, and it is rarely easy. Naomi's grief temporarily blinded her to Ruth's value. Sometimes pain makes it hard to see what God has placed right next to us. But God does not withdraw His hand just because we can't feel it.

Maybe you're in a 'Naomi season,' where everything feels like loss and bitterness, where what you once held dear is now buried in grief. And maybe, like Naomi, you don't see the Ruth beside you. Maybe you're missing the fact that God has already started to answer your prayer, even before it was formed on your lips. Don't dismiss the people who stay when you try to push them away. Don't ignore the small signs of favor that whisper, *"You're not forgotten."* Take courage, God is never late, and He is never unprepared.

Prayer: God's Pattern of Provision

Faithful Father,

You are the one who sees before I know what I'll need. The one who weaves provision into my path, not always with fanfare but with purpose. Thank You for being a Provider, not just of things, but of peace, purpose, and presence. In Jesus' Name. Amen.

Reflection Question

Can you identify a time when God provided for you in an unexpected way?

Journal Your Thoughts

_____

_____

_____

_____

_____

_____

_____

_____

_____

CHAPTER EIGHT

GOD IN THE GLEANING

"So she went out, entered a field and began to glean behind the harvesters. As it turned out, she was working in a field belonging to Boaz..."
Ruth 2:3 (NIV)

God doesn't always lead us with a loud voice. Sometimes He guides us with quiet providence through open doors we didn't knock on, fields we didn't plan to walk in, and moments we didn't expect to matter. That's what happened to Ruth. She "happened" to glean in a field that belonged to Boaz. But in God's kingdom, nothing is random. What looks like a coincidence to us is often divine coordination.

That truth became real for me recently. I felt directionless. I wasn't looking for destiny, just simply strength and reason to get out of bed each morning. I felt numb. But, like Ruth, I kept moving. I showed up. I did what was in front of me, even if it felt small. And in doing so, I began to see that God meets us in the field of the ordinary.

In the midst of what we endure, God is still present. Healing doesn't always come in a flash. Sometimes it shows up in the gleaning. What do I mean? Sometimes healing shows up in the daily rhythms of obedience and in the quiet decisions to keep going. Ruth went out day after day to pick up leftover grain, not realizing she was walking into destiny! I continued day after day in ministry, prayer, and writing, coupled with my weekly therapy sessions, not recognizing that those small steps were sowing seeds of healing in my heart.

The field where Ruth gleaned was also the place where God was preparing her future. Sometimes, the very places where you feel overlooked (those unseen corners of faithfulness) are the fields where God will begin to rewrite your own story.

What I love about this part of Ruth's journey is that God didn't change everything overnight. Naomi was still grieving. Ruth was still poor. But something had shifted. God was now visibly moving, placing Ruth in the path of Boaz, a redeemer. And Naomi, who once said the Lord had made her life bitter, would soon begin to see the glimmers of hope again.

Maybe that's where you are, where Ruth was, just gleaning, just surviving. But I want to encourage you, don't despise your field. Keep showing up, no matter how uncomfortable or pointless it seems. Keep gathering what you can, because God is building a future during what feels like fragments.

Prayer: God in the Gleaning

Dear Lord,

When I feel small, tired, and overlooked, anchor my soul in the truth: You are in my every step, every sheaf, every silent moment of obedience. You are God in the gleaning, faithful, generous, and near. In Jesus' Name. Amen.

Reflection Question

What small, overlooked places in your life has God used to reveal His presence and faithfulness, and how can you begin to see the 'gleanings' as grace?

Journal Your Thoughts

CHAPTER NINE

FINDING LOVE AGAIN

"As she got up to glean, Boaz gave orders to his men: 'Let her gather among the sheaves and don't reprimand her. Even pull out some stalks for her from the bundles and leave them for her to pick up, and don't rebuke her."
Ruth 2:15-16 (NIV)

Grief has a way of robbing your ability to love, but Naomi would find love again. Not through a new marriage, but through the faithfulness of Ruth, the integrity of Boaz, and the redeeming hand of God.

Boaz provided food, protection, and respect for Ruth, a woman society had every reason to ignore. He didn't just bless Ruth; he blessed Naomi. Naomi's love story wasn't about romance; it was about redemption. It was about being seen again, cared for again, and restored again. This is what God's love looks like in our grief: quiet, consistent, and redemptive.

In ancient Israel, widows like Naomi had no legal claim to their deceased husbands' land. It would pass to the nearest male relative unless a kinsman-redeemer stepped in to reclaim the land and carry on the family name. Boaz was one such relative. When Naomi guided Ruth to ask Boaz to "spread his garment" over her (a symbolic act requesting redemption), Boaz could have acted impulsively. But instead, he honored the law to actively redeem them.

But here we find a challenge: there was a nearer relative who had the first right to redeem the land and marry Ruth. Boaz went to the gate of the city, a place where justice was rendered, covenants were publicly affirmed, and legal matters were settled. He gathered ten elders and presented the case clearly and publicly.
The nearer relative declined, unwilling to bear the cost of redemption, but Boaz was willing.

Boaz at the gate presents a beautiful picture of Jesus, our Kinsman-Redeemer, who stands publicly to redeem those who were outsiders. He married Ruth, not just out of affection, but out of a lawful act of restoration. And in doing so, he redeemed both Ruth and Naomi. This act was the resurrection of a broken lineage, and a public declaration that Naomi's family still mattered.

Boaz did not cut corners. He fulfilled every legal requirement to ensure that Ruth and Naomi were not only loved but also lawfully redeemed.

Jesus, our Redeemer, went to all extremes to save you and me:

- He fulfilled every legal requirement of righteousness.

- He didn't bypass the Law, He satisfied it (see Romans 8:3-4).

- He faced the public shame of the cross to secure our inheritance.

- He paid the full price, not with barley or silver, but with His own blood (see Hebrews 9:12).

And like Boaz, Jesus didn't redeem one person. He redeemed grieving humanity: broken, bitter, and hopeless. He restored us to joy and hope.

God's love doesn't always come as we imagine. It may not arrive in the form of a spouse, a financial breakthrough, or a perfect life. His love often blooms in the soil of our deepest grief. For the woman who feels too old, wounded, or forgotten, Naomi's story is yours, too.

Prayer For Finding Love Again

Loving Lord,

You are the Author of love, not just the first time, but every time after. Though I may be unsettled in my grief, teach me that love is not over. I know that because You are not finished with me. In Jesus' Name. Amen.

Reflection Question

After loss or heartbreak, what fears or doubts have made it hard for you to receive love again?

Journal Your Thoughts

CHAPTER TEN

GOD'S FAVOR AND DELIVERANCE

"And he said, 'Who are you?' So she answered, 'I am Ruth, your maidservant under your wing, for you are a close relative.'"
Ruth 3:9 (ESV)

When we hear the word "favor," we often picture elevation; lavish blessings, doors swinging open, opportunities we never imagined, and a life that looks enviable from the outside. But in Naomi's story, we encounter a different kind of favor; one that's shaped in the shadows, the wilderness of grief, scarcity, and uncertainty. God's favor doesn't always glitter. Sometimes it groans.

Naomi's story intrigues me because she suffers immeasurable loss due to famine, migration, and the deaths of her husband and sons. Now you tell me, what kind of favor is that? If we judged God's favor only by external comfort, we could classify Naomi as cursed, not blessed. Her name change to "Mara" justifies that she believed that God's hand had turned against her. Yet in the ashes of her pain, God was rewriting her story; one of redemption, hope, and deliverance.

Ruth chose to remain with Naomi and clung to a God she barely knew, forsaking her homeland for a future she could neither see nor imagine. They journeyed back to Bethlehem, broken and unsure. But God's favor had already gone before them. It walked with them through chaos and led them into deliverance.

I have learned that the favor of God is not the absence of struggle; it is often His presence during the struggle. Too often, we want God's favor to deliver us *from* hardship. But God often delivers us *through* hardship. Ruth and Naomi were not spared the valley, but they were not alone in it. Their deliverance came step by step, woven into everyday obedience and divine encounters.

Who would've thought that two widows in a strange land, scrapping for barley in a foreign field, were part of the divine plan to bring forth the Messiah?

That is the mystery of God's favor: it doesn't always make sense in the moment. It can look like lack, a delay, or even despair. But behind the curtain of chaos, God is crafting something holy, and you're a part of it.

When you find yourself in the middle of hardship, facing unanswered prayers, closed doors, or silent seasons, remember Naomi's story. God was working, even when it seemed like He wasn't. His favor may not always be fast. But it is indeed faithful.

Let's re-purpose our minds and not limit favor to what we can flaunt. Let's recognize it in the grace to keep going, in the people who stand with us, and in the redemption that comes in quiet, persistent ways. For in the story of Naomi we don't just find favor, but the one who holds favor in His hands, the Redeemer Himself.

Prayer For God's Favor and Deliverance

Almighty Redeemer,

You are the God who sees me in famine and leads me into harvest. You are the God who sits with me in sorrow and walks with me into songs of joy. Cover me with Your favor. Surround me with Your deliverance. Let my testimony be that You still rescue, You still redeem, and You still restore. In the mighty name of Jesus. Amen.

Reflection Question

When has God's favor shown up in your life in a way that didn't feel like favor at first?

Journal Your Thoughts

_____

_____

_____

_____

_____

_____

_____

_____

CHAPTER ELEVEN

A GRIEVING MOTHER'S LEGACY

*"Naomi took the baby and cuddled him to her breast.
And she cared for him as if he were her own."*
Ruth 4:16 (NLT)

God can take a grieving woman, a bitter soul, and a broken family and still write a happy ending. What a God! She didn't get there by striving. She didn't manipulate her way back into blessing. She simply returned, empty, honest, and wounded. And God met her there.

Let's talk legacy for a moment. Naomi became the grandmother of Obed, the great-grandmother of Jesse, and the great-great-grandmother of King David. From her line would eventually come Jesus Christ, the Redeemer of all. This process wasn't instant, but redemptive. This grieving widow in Moab became the mother of the Messiah's line.

Here's the beauty in all of this: God can use grief in a marvelous way, if it is surrendered to Him. If you have ever made a decision that led you to a "Moab," a place you knew was not where God intended; if you have ever grieved losses so great that you renamed yourself "bitter"; if you've wondered whether God could do anything with what's left of your life, let Naomi's experiences whisper these truths into your soul:

- You are not too far gone.
- You are not too broken.
- You are not forgotten.

God can birth a legacy from your grief and deliver you, even after your disobedience.

Prayer For A Grieving Mother's Legacy

Merciful Savior,

You see me, not just as a woman grieving, but as a mother carrying a legacy I cannot yet fully see. I am Yours, even in my sorrow, even in my silence, even as I wait. In Jesus' Name. Amen.

Reflection Question

What legacy is grief shaping in you, and how might your pain become a testimony that blesses generations after you?

Journal Your Thoughts

___

___

___

___

___

___

___

___

___

CHAPTER TWELVE

THE WITNESS OF SACRED SCARS

"Then the women of the town said to Naomi, "Praise the LORD, who has now provided a redeemer for your family! May this child be famous in Israel. May he restore your youth and care for you in your old age. For he is the son of your daughter-in-law who loves you and has been better to you than seven sons!"
Ruth 4:14-15 (NLT)

Naomi never preached a sermon. She never penned a Psalm. She didn't call fire down from heaven or part the sea. Yet her story became sacred because she survived and was willing to walk the long road home. Some of the strongest people I know never shout their story from a stage. But they all had one thing in common, they carried their pain with quiet grace, silently sowing tears that no one sees. I was one of them, breaking inside, grieving deeply, and fighting for my sanity on days I had to hold it together while living in a new country.

The scars I carry today are not signs of weakness; I have finally accepted that they are sacred and that they are my witnesses to you. They are reminders that grief did not and will not win; that life tried to hollow me out, but God filled me instead. He didn't always remove my pain, but He rechanneled it. He gave my pain purpose. He didn't always answer my questions when I wanted them answered, but He held me through the silence of it all.

Sometimes we look at our losses and long for what was. But grief can't always be reversed. Some chapters end. Some people leave. Some people pass on. Some things don't get fixed. And yet, redemption means that even in what we cannot change, God can birth new beginnings.

I didn't get all the answers, but I got stronger. I have by no means mastered this process of grief; I still struggle with the effects of death and sudden loss, but now, I have found healing in hidden places. I am learning to breathe through ache and to sing despite the silence. I simply call that sacred strength.

So if you're carrying your grief quietly, know that you are seen. Your faithfulness in the shadows matters. Your survival is a testimony. And your scars (those sacred reminders) are evidence that resurrection is still possible.

Prayer For the Witness of Sacred Scars

Healing God,

You are the Keeper of every wound I survived. Use my story, my sorrow, and my scars for Your glory. In Jesus' Name. Amen.

Reflection Question

What scars do you carry that once brought shame or silence, but now speak of God's grace?

Journal Your Thoughts

_____

_____

Adiese Jonas-Murphy

CHAPTER THIRTEEN

BEAUTY AFTER 'MARA'

"The neighbor women said, "Now at last Naomi has a son again!" And they named him Obed. He became the father of Jesse and the grandfather of David."
Ruth 4:17 (NLT)

Let's do a quick recap.

Naomi's journey began with famine, followed by death, displacement, and deep sorrow. She returned to Bethlehem bitter, convinced that the Almighty had afflicted her, and her story was finished. But Ruth stayed, Boaz stepped in, and God, well, He rewrote the whole ending.

We have now reached the final moments of her story, and yes, she is a grandmother of promise. She is also a beauty that rises out of 'Mara.' The women in Bethlehem proclaimed, *"Naomi has a son!"* as if to say her legacy had died. The emptiness she once wore like a cloak had been replaced by the fullness of new life.

This is what God does best. He takes our 'bitter' and brings 'beauty.' I'm sure you have had to pass through some bitter experiences, but understand that God was weaving something beautiful, something you are yet to see. God isn't trying to destroy you in this season. He is rebuilding you. You will be stronger. You will be healed.

I still carry the memories of Dad. I see his undeniable forehead and even expressions in my children every single day. I still feel the tug of grief in quiet moments when I reflect on all that I have endured in a short time span. But what once felt like the end has now become a doorway. What once felt like shame has become one of my greatest testimonies. What was bitterness has now become beauty, not because the pain disappeared, but because God transformed it.

This journey has taught me:

- That a new beginning is sometimes disguised in sorrow.

- A fresh chapter often takes its cue from disappointment.

- A resurrection is most often catapulted from loss.

You may not be holding your "Obed" just yet (the tangible evidence of your restoration), but don't give up. Keep walking. Keep gleaning. Keep returning. Because God still writes beautiful endings. And when He does, you'll find yourself cradling joy in your arms as evidence that you have survived, that grace has sustained you, and that your journey back was worth it all.

Prayer: Beauty After Mara

Redeeming God,

You saw me when I renamed myself "Mara." You held me when the bitterness of grief clouded every glimpse of hope. You heard my cries when I could no longer pretend to be whole. When others look at my life, let them see beauty after Mara, because there is a God after grief. In the name of the Restorer of All Things, Jesus Christ. Amen.

Reflection Question

In what ways has your experience of loss revealed unexpected beauty?

Journal Your Thoughts

ABOUT THE AUTHOR

Adiese Jonas-Murphy is a speaker, author, media consultant, and woman of deep faith who knows the language of grief firsthand.

After walking through the painful loss of her father, her mother's stroke, her sister's near-death experience, and her in-laws' battles with stage four cancer in quick succession, Adiese discovered that God's faithfulness doesn't erase sorrow, but it redeems it. Through the lens of biblical storytelling, prayer, and deep reflection on the Word of God, she empowers others to rise from their broken places and return to hope.

Professional Experience

Adiese's professional experience is characterized by extensive roles in **Mass Media** and **Communications leadership.** She launched her career in 2008 at Power 106FM and Music 99FM, demonstrating versatility in creative and technical functions, including working as a

Senior Creative Assistant, Duty Announcer, News Presenter, and the Producer of the morning talk show *Independent Talk with Ronnie Thwaites*.

Furthermore, she showcased her production and voice talent as the Writer, Producer, and Voice for the children's gospel feature, *"The Pickney Corner,"* aired on the program *Power and Glory*. After this foundational media experience, she transitioned into a communications leadership role, serving as the Assistant Communication Director for the East Jamaica Conference from October 2010 to October 2013, solidifying her expertise in managing organizational messaging and outreach.

Her career progressed significantly when she was invited to join the Northern Caribbean University (NCU) Media Group in November 2013, encompassing NCU TV and Radio, where she undertook several senior administrative and public-facing roles. Her positions included Marketing Manager, Programmes Manager, and Assistant Director of Corporate Communications, Marketing and Public Relations. During this tenure, she also served as a broadcast personality, co-hosting several programs on NCU FM, most notably *Sunset Serenade, a program co-hosted with her husband for 9 years.*

Building on this leadership, she was later appointed as the Associate Communication Director for the West Jamaica Conference of SDA, where she managed oversight of the local cable station, WCCN. Complementing her hands-on media and executive communications experience, she has also contributed to vocational education by teaching and lecturing part-time at the Heart College of Innovation and Technology in Montego Bay.

Her career achievements are further underscored by several prestigious awards, including:

- Most Outstanding Technical Worker (WJC)- *awarded by the Jamaica Union Conference of Seventh-day Adventists in 2017.*
- Best Producer's Award (EJC) for 2021- 2022 *awarded by the East Jamaica Conference of Seventh-day Adventists.*
- President's Leadership Award for COVID-19 2020-2022 *awarded by the Jamaica Union Conference of Seventh-day Adventists.*
- The Top Producer's Award for East Jamaica Conference 2020-2022 *awarded by the Jamaica Union Conference of Seventh-day Adventists.*

She is the founder of SetALite Media and remains the heart behind several Christian productions, publications, and programs.

Titles aside, she adores being the wife of Darren and mother to Zachary and Dominique.

Adiese enjoys faithfully ministering to her congregants and sharing the love of Christ with others.

www.ingramcontent.com/pod-product-compliance
Lightning Source LLC
Chambersburg PA
CBHW050704160426
43194CB00010B/1991